Father Light

Poetic voices of fatherhood

Blossom & Berry

Copyright © 2020 Blossom & Berry
All rights reserved.
ISBN:

This book is a collection of poetic voices on love, light and fatherhood created with courage and vulnerability.

"The definition of vulnerability is uncertainty, risk, and emotional exposure. But vulnerability is not weakness; it's our most accurate measure of courage. When the barrier is our belief about vulnerability, the question becomes: Are we willing to show up and be seen when we can't control the outcome? When the barrier to vulnerability is about safety, the question becomes: Are we willing to create courageous spaces so we can be fully seen? A soft and open front is not being weak; it's being brave, it's being the wilderness."

- *Brené Brown, Braving The Wilderness.*

Foreword by Mark Williams

Father Light is one of the first books to bring poetry and the importance of fatherhood and mental health to the fore.

After the success of Mother Light and the work Gayle has done, I am delighted to be asked to say a few words from a new father who himself suffered in silence for many years.

This book is a very powerful book of poems which we hope will encourage more fathers to share their own journeys, through poetry, a proactive activity that can help share those feelings that are often not shared amongst new parents. The book will also open up these kinds of conversations and, we hope, encourage other fathers to seek help for themselves if they need it, to benefit their families and also benefit their child's development.

I am also very happy that the donations will benefit the Hub Of Hope which is a database of services that new fathers can access, and with many such services now starting to provide important support, it's an exciting time for the book to be released.

As a father who witnessed a traumatic birth, and with my wonderful wife Michelle suffering from severe anxiety and depression after the birth of our son Ethan, I suffered in silence with anxiety and depression in the post-natal period.

I didn't know any other fathers who talked about these unwanted feelings. At the same time, I felt very guilty about feelings that I had never experienced before in my life, after struggling at first to bond with my son. The first year of fatherhood was the most lonely for me. I had deep feelings of isolation and I could not tell Michelle how I was feeling as I didn't want to worsen her mental health. I couldn't even tell my closest friends.

This, of course, showed in changes to my personality. I started avoiding situations whilst using poor coping skills which were harming myself. I know now that the quicker a person seeks help, the quicker their recovery.

Gayle's book would have certainly made me understand that any new parents can struggle during this time. The biggest killer in men under fifty is suicide, so it's really important to seek help before it gets to crisis point.

Reports suggest that up to 39 per cent of new fathers struggle with their mental health and up to fifty per cent of fathers can experience depression when looking after a partner with post-natal depression. This book will be another important resource for new fathers, especially as there are so few publications around at this important time. The human mind can only process about five to seven pieces of information at any one time, and poetry, therefore, can be processed very easily. Processing information is even harder when you are dealing with depression, so again, poetry can be a very powerful source of comfort and expression.

Another benefit of poetry, and this book, is that it gives you permission to search the depths of your soul and to write what is happening underneath the surface. I personally find it easier to write my thoughts down rather than keep them suppressed in my mind.

Father Light could help health and mental health professionals to more easily include fathers by sharing the experiences of other men in the same position as them - fathers, at a time when new fathers are often forgotten. So I am very excited that this book is now published and believe it will help this generation and generations to come.

Mark Williams – International campaigner, author and keynote speaker.

Dada, unrefined

Begin: What will you look like? What will I do?

Then I first see you cry. Strained pink face.

No, not a cry. It's a soft plea.

"Protect" says dull dada.

A tribal instinct, latent, now active.

One side kind, the other, crude and defensive.

I'd give you the whole world if I could.

I'll scorch the whole world if I need to.

You're my first kid. What do?

How many months to walk? To read? To swing alone?

How many months until you can ace the LSAT?

I see every odd decision as you grow.

Sometimes I fear you will be Forrest Gump.

30 years old and finger-painting.

I'll love you anyway.

Then you surprise me. You can spell a

Little bit. You can logic a little bit.

Now I feel competitive and a little scared.

I see myself through you. Stop copying me!

My stern expressions. My playful core.

I like Star Wars, so of course, you too.

Pause. Reassess. Who will my child mirror today?

I get lazy and sometimes angry.

No girl, not all men are like that.

But right now, they are to you.

You see every odd decision as I grow.

My joke that made three-year-old you laugh.

And four-year-old you correct me.

My attempt to discipline which fossilized

your defiance. Dismissing my decades of

wisdom for your 60 months of certainty.

Don't get cocky, kid.

Continue: What keeps me up is not

That you will cry or rush down the wrong path.

Forget the cowardly, comforting conceit

of a pain-free life, where growth is a myth.

Nah. What makes me sweat is that one day

I won't be there. And I can't be your force ghost.

Keep copying me. Internalize. Trial and error.

That's my only hope of ensuring you're never alone.

Tony Harris

The Journey into Fatherhood

After the most beautiful and natural process of labour and birth (well done to my amazing partner Emma and all of you other mums – it's truly phenomenal), my beautiful baby girl was born at 06:49 on 21st April 2020 – Our lockdown baby. What a moment!

Now onto fatherhood ... Honestly? The first three days of being home were like a dream world, but it soon hit me like a train. A train of realisation that this was my new life.

Was I as prepared as I thought?

Nowhere near.

The painful and sickening night feeds.

The burps.

The colic.

The reflux.

I needed to adapt and adapt quick. Of course, it didn't happen overnight - it took a few months. For a few months, I lacked connection, closeness and love.

Instead, I had feelings of resentment and saw my new baby girl as a burden and an inconvenience.

Why do I feel like this?

Why am I not connecting?

Do I need help?

It's clear to me now, I potentially had post-natal depression (the daddy version).

The fake smile or fake nod when other people would say, "Isn't it amazing being a dad?"

Slowly but surely, though, things began to change. I began connecting, the closeness developed, the love grew and now we are inseparable. Six months on and the pride, love and joy I feel every single day is indescribable and a true blessing.

So for any new fathers or fathers-to-be who can relate or take something from this, my advice would be to be honest about your feelings, speak up, seek help or simply give time.

It will be worth it.

Chris Quinn (The, now, extremely proud father of Ariah Rose).

Three years later

For Alice and Henry

Watching my coffee go cold in an Asda on the outskirts of nowhere,

Killing time waiting on the car,

Reflecting on 3 years as a Dad,

Now with two instead of one.

Back then I was so naive,

Thinking it would be hard,

Because that's what everyone says,

Without any real understanding of what that meant.

Ecstatic at the birth of our first,

Then joy faded and fear reigned,

Fear that I might get it all wrong and ruin their life,

When I now know that getting it wrong is just a part of being a Dad.

It felt like starting a new full time job,

One that you loved more than anything,

But with no training or manual you're on your own,

Three years on and I'm starting to master the basics.

I never realised how diverse it would be being a dad,

I've become the explainer of everything,

Answering why for the hundredth time,

All while acting as lord protector of plug sockets from the onslaught of our youngest.

It's taken an emotional toll,

Memories of my children crying because I had to go away,

Wanting to abandon the trip,

To just spend another ten minutes with them.

However, after three years I still love being a Dad,

I walk in after work to a child at my midriff and one chewing my leg,

Their love makes me a better person,

My love I hope will make them one too.

David Cooper

Three to Four to Now

When you arrived it made us a three

Happiness, love, the bond was plain to see.

When you cried, we rocked and cuddled

When you laughed, I burst with joy.

Then you arrived and made us a four

No problem, we've done this before!

Milk was not easy and oh how you cried.

You only wanted mummy, no matter what I tried

But over time this all softened, something very special blossomed.

Now, the bond is strong between us four

So much more than I'd hoped for

Forged through persistence and lots of learning

Love and laughter now recurring.

To Cameron and Rowan

Lots of Love

Daddy

Xxx

Alex Smith

The Guidance

So what's the deal?
It's a steal
It's the way it makes you feel
It's the way it helps you heal.

My daughter tells me I help her be responsible
She doesn't know that's exactly how I stay responsible
They make anything possible
She says that's why we have a hospital.

Sometimes you need to let go and let them grow
Only they can discover what we know
And they show us the things we don't know
Enabling us to grow
And showing us we don't have to run the whole show.

The look that says I need your help
Gardening in the dirt
Helping Mollie with her homework,
arts and crafts, cooking and baking.

Now the real deal
Admitting when I'm wrong
That's how I show her how to be strong

Unconditional means allowing them to be wrong.

That moment when they call for us

To witness what's making their life more interesting

So the deal that's made with another human being is the bestest deal

I have felt real pain and have shed some tears

But they're moments short-lived

With the rest

I've been privileged with over the years.

Growing together

The guidance for each other.

Mark McCormack

The Carrying Of The Light-For Otis Kemp

Redundant expectations for you I have not in mind

Such ideas are of a kind that I know better than to entertain

'Tis a foolish father to his own self-disdain to dictate the path of such arrows

Try to cheat the math of the universe's beautiful game, I proclaim,

The man you shall become is of your own will and judgment.

Simple words instead, I offer to you my son, should I abruptly depart

And you remain again to start and face the world in its profound apparition

To establish your position in the cavalcade, to elect yang or yin, honor or sin

Woe betide those ignorant of the darkness within, that twists its wicked plot

Those whom forgot, the provenance of evil is tantamount to that of their virtue.

In those times where the road is not clear and you cannot find your way

Embrace the torment of that troubled day, for it hides the true teaching of life

Existence without obstacle or strife is simply inhibition of the flower's growth

Treasure the impediments and freedoms both, for both are peas in a pod

Even omnipotent formless God lacks the limitation of which we fortuitously inhabit.

Delight in the plentifulness of the many, see the dance of nature in all its array

Though stay your heart to recognize that it is but a dance of fiction in form

Manifested in the outward burst of geometric adornment and miracle

Everything is but one, all is the same beneath, belief in the other an illusion

A necessary amusement for the sake of your story, a me, a my, to live, to die.

Let love flow through you like the breaking of a dam and echo all around

Do what you can, for all you can, it is that very love that maketh the man

Speak only what you know to be true, for the universe knows when you don't

I vow, karma won't forsake your plight, behave with honor, do what is right

Despite the consequences, for you are your own judge, you are carrying the light.

It is gratitude, not thanklessness that will bring you abundant joy

Be thankful for creation, try not to destroy what opportunity has brought

See how we fought over yang, over yin, to lose or to win for this existence herein,

Yes you will want that the black fold to white, that wrong yield to right, its but dualistic intent

Hell-bent on the things for which our ego yearns, learn this, it is all here and now

Allow it to be, surrender and see that the universe is not what it would first seem.

...find the answer within, awaken from the dream.

Ryan Michael Kemp

Feelings of a Father

I feel guilt when I have to leave

I feel guilt when I can't be with you

The feeling slowly imprisons my soul,

Then I look into your crystal clear eyes

It soothes my guilt filled mind,

As I see the forgiveness and your organic love.

You are my soul and you're my life

You'll outgrow my lap but never my heart

I'll always hold your hand even when I'm not there

Just look into your heart you'll find me there, forever

We're tied to each other with a special bond,

Called Daddy and Daughter love.

Tamas Dominko

Sonnet for Violet

You're part of your mum and part of me,

You beat at the heart of our small family.

We waited nine months to finally meet you,

And when you arrived, I was so glad to greet you.

I do a good job, keep you safe, fed and clean,

Yet I can also be grumpy and snappy and mean.

You're so precious and perfect – the apple of our eye,

Yet sometimes, I just make you cry.

You love spending time with your grumpy old dad,

But sometimes I want to go out with the lads.

You won't be little forever – you grow every day,

Soon you'll be grown and flying away.

So I'll try my best to be better, all the better to prove,

I'm a dad who is worthy of his daughter's love.

Peter Traynor

Sleep well my son

It's not about pointing fingers,

It's not about who is to blame.

It's not about feeling guilty,

And it's not about feeling the shame.

Your demons are gone forever,

You're now in a safer place.

If only you'd shared your torment,

Such things you couldn't face.

Sleep well my son forever,

We'll meet again one day.

I'll cherish our time together,

And see your son along his way.

Chris Jones

When She arrived, I was not surprised, to not know what to do

I did things wrong, but we mugged along and I learnt as we played.

The night shifts ended and I pretended that we had got it all worked out

but when He arrived, I realised, I did not have a clue!

The things I knew, tricks I'd learnt, did not work on him

He was new, brand brand new, and He was not the same.

She did this, but He did that and I almost went insane.

It took a year, a full 12 months, for me to work it out

to look on him, to understand, to love him to the brim.

Things began to settle down, routine was near worked out

but it wasn't long before their brother came along

then chaos ruled throughout!

16 years have passed since then and he and him are almost men

She is the blossom of this Berry- and beautiful, like her Mum

I'm not sure what it is I did, to win three wonderful first-prizes.

But I've come to learn that as a Dad, life is full of big surprises.

Jolyon Berry

You and Me

There's no easy way to say quite what you mean to me,
I've never been too good with words so, let's see.

I suppose that I could talk about my endless love for You,
And tell of all the games we play and silly things we do.

We sing, we dance, have so much fun, I couldn't ask for more,
There's so many things about You, Little One, I adore.

You make me a better person and help me through my struggles,
You lift me up when I'm sad, with kindness, hugs and cuddles.

And though I'm here to teach You how to do the little things,
You teach me so much more what pride and joy it brings!

I might not be the perfect Daddy, but I always try to be,
I think when we're together we're a good team, You and me.

One day you'll be grown up, but things won't change, we'll still be silly,
You'll always be a star, and we'll still be You and Me.

Rob Sime

A Couple of Things

To my dear Thing One,

I've got one important thing to say,
One thing you need to hear today.
You see, what I would like to say,
In a clear and simple way is
Thing One, I love you.

And now, my dear Thing Two,

Without further ado,
I've two important things for you.
One thing (as I said to Thing One too) is
Thing Two, I love you.
The next is simply thank you, for being my Thing Two.

Rob Sime

The Path

The path of the mother is steep and harsh, requiring a swift and exhausting ascent.

The path of the father meanders through the swampy lowlands of the man-child, too often have pilgrims lost their way and become mired. Don't lose sight of the route, the journey is ever more fascinating, and the destination is worth the surrender of every one of your childish ways.

Bob Newton

#HowAreYouDad?

Fatherhood is an incredible journey full of surprises but also a roller coaster of emotions which can overwhelm us with feelings that sometimes do not come to the surface.

Fatherhood gives us purpose but on the other hand self-doubt our abilities to be the best version we want to be as a dad.

Fatherhood can bring wonderful experiences and but can also make us over-think and pressure us to be this perfect father, which does not exist.

Fatherhood has changed in recent years while services have not caught up with the times which can impact on our lives and the whole family around us.

Fatherhood changes our lives for the better but can be an isolating and lonely time which can impact on our mental and physical health.

Fatherhood beliefs are different in every dad, some are traditional, and some are not, while learned sometimes through our own fathers.

Fatherhood can bring us happiness and a higher responsibility to provide for the people we care about the most in our lives.

Fatherhood brings all those happy feelings that Motherhood brings while also those feelings of guilt, worry, intrusive thoughts, extreme stress, anxieties, depression and low self-esteem as a parent

Fatherhood has shaped me as a person and provided me with a passion to help other fathers struggling during this time. So next time your brother, friend, or someone you may know is entering Fatherhood, please ask the simple question How Are You Dad and listen.

Mark Williams

I was a child once

I was a child once.

I was a child once, you know?

I know it was quite a while ago.

Like every adult alive I started as a baby and grew

to be this older human in front of you.

But having a child now that I'm a dad.

Has wiped the disc of all the memories I had

It's ... we have never experienced life as a young human being.

It's like we just appeared with all our adult bits and began seeing

Life through older eyes.

It's all a great surprise.

The phases they go through are new.

We are useless, flummoxed, unsure of what to do.

How to react. How to control. How to guide.

Where has this little being come from? Where did he hide?

I've never experienced this before.

Tantrums. Terrible two's. First day at school. Can't take much more.

And worse it gets. The pile of toys gets higher. I see new things I've never seen.

Too little sleep. No date nights. Our time's not ours. And now they are teens!

Can't understand how it all came about, this change in how we live.

It's not natural. It's sinful. It's so hard. We just give, give, give.

Can't understand these little kids. From where did they come? Where will they go?

I was a child once, you know.

Paddy McMahon

I Now Understand

You will never understand the love of a child until you have one yourself.

You will never understand the bond between a child and their father.

You will never understand the struggle the mother goes through.

You will never understand that having step-children can give you a unique bond identical to your own children.

I see my daughters' eyes look at me for the first time, relying on me, trusting me and loving me, now I understand.

When my daughters hold me tight and tell me how much I mean to them, now I understand.

To see a woman go through so much pain for the perfect end result, now I understand.

My step-sons are my sons and only blood separates our unique bond, I now understand.

I now understand that being a father is the best job in the world.

I now understand being a father is my greatest achievement.

I now understand that my step-sons consider me their best friend.

For all the mothers, it's fair to say I now understand.

Aaron Wendell Willis

Fatherhood

My life changed the moment I saw your heart beat flickering on the screen.

That unexplainable source of energy.

That miracle called life.

A plethora of emotions holding you in my arms for the first time, avalanching with such intensity that I felt my heart would burst with joy.

Hours upon hours observing your every move, every sound, jumping and dashing, panicking with the inexperience of fatherhood, snarling like an overprotecting lion at every perceived danger. Simultaneously, gazing into these deep blue eyes, watching me with innocent curiosity and love.

Finally closing my eyes and resting my forehead peacefully on yours, finding nothing but calmness and serenity like drifting gently on a motionless ocean. My favourite waste of time.

At the blink of an eye, the baby is gone and you've grown into this little girl, full of joy and wonder and a million questions. Sensitive and kind, funny and smart, like a delicate flower, complex and beautiful. A thoughtful soul completely in tune with its heart.

My love and pride for you grows and grows, day by day, as I start to see the foundations of the woman you will become. I want to help you, protect you and take away your fears and self-doubts, and help you believe in you the way I do. For I see the "You" before you can see "Her" yourself.

Countless moments of pure happiness like never before experienced, watching you grow and laugh and finding your path in this beautiful new world. Making my heart sing with rapture.

Finally, a sense of purpose.

Paolo Pelizzari

Gift from God

You meet the woman of your dreams,

You fall in love,

Your love grows as each day passes,

You buy a house, a car,

All the things to create a life together,

Then you become a Dad,

But this is different, it's a special love,

A special gift,

It's a gift from God.

You hear your baby cry,

You have sleepless nights,

But your love still grows as each day passes,

Before your very eyes,

Your baby has grown from,

A little girl into a beautiful young lady,

It's a precious privilege,

The best gift ever,

It's a gift from God.

You bear witness to the cycle of life and love,

Your child's love story begins,

She finds love, the man of her dreams,

Her love grows as each day passes,

She gets married, buys a house,

And you watch as her life takes its own path,

She becomes a Mother,

Loves her child unconditionally,

And experiences the precious privilege,

It's a gift for her from God.

Now I'm a Grandad,

And my love for my granddaughter is boundless,

I'll spend my days, months and years,

Watching my little princess growing,

Slowly into a young beautiful lady,

And witness my daughter watch,

As her daughter begins her own adventure,

Becoming a Dad is an honour,

But becoming a Grandad is priceless,

It's love, it's life, it's us, it's special,

It truly is a gift from God.

Bharat Chauhan

Fatherhood

Ain't all it's cracked up to be,

Sleepless nights,

Dirty nappies,

Tears and tantrums,

Pretending you're happy,

Doing your best,

Never enough,

Boss don't care,

Wife simply indifferent to your internal struggles,

Groups for mums, mums get depression,

Dads simply expected to handle the pressure,

I mean,

It's not manly, is it?

Car is fucked, grass needs cutting, kid number one looks like a vagrant,

Shirts to iron, dinners to cook,

Daughter won't take a bottle, just wants a tit,

Everything,

Literally everything,

Going to shit.

Gotta be strong, gotta be fresh from the fight,

But I just want my slouch pants and a beer,

And to hear,

That I'm doing alright,

I mean I think I am? I hope I am? Tell me I am?

But I haven't seen my friends in six months,

Forgotten they exist in a whirlwind of Ella's Kitchen,

And jabs for rubella, measels and mumps,

Who the fuck gets mumps now anyway?

Now it's all Roblox and Minecraft and Fifa 2020,

Dinner time, bathtime, bedtime, storytime,

What about daddy's fucking time?

Muddy shoes, dirty car, food on the floor,

Shit in the bath,

Again.

School uniforms,

Packed lunches.

Hair gel on the eldest,

Looking like a nine-year old Elvis,

But then,

It's holding hands,

It's I love you daddy

It's looking into their eyes,

Knowing you're the most important person they know,

Knowing that you would do anything for them,

It's late night cuddles,

It's 6am starts on a Saturday when they crawl under your duvet,

It's football in the park,

It's wobbly teeth,

It's grazed knees and bike rides,

Catching fish and flying kites,

It's celebrating a late goal together,

It's their successes, their failures,

All the terrible Christmas plays they were in,

It's everything. You're everything.

The best job in the world,

Fatherhood.

P. Hart

Daddy To Gray

When I was 18 years old, I fell pregnant with Gray.

Falling pregnant was a massive surprise. I had no plans for children. I was terrified but so excited to have my little family.

It had been scary enough coming out as transgender as a teenager. But when I cut my hair and changed my name, it was the first time I felt free.

I was even more scared about sharing my news with friends and family: wondering what they would think about me carrying and birthing a child.

Being his Dad.

I had a perception of how people might react. People are curious, and I am happy to answer questions. But sometimes their words are said with the intention to hurt. I try to laugh in those moments.

I feel lucky to have had so much support stepping into my pregnancy.

To all the doctors and nurses who didn't misgender me and called me Dad: thank you. You were amazing with your support for me as a pregnant man.

"The first man to give birth in the Women's Hospital."

Holding my son for the first time was such a beautiful moment but so scary. I was holding him and all I can remember is being terrified.

"He is mine and I have to look after him!"

Parenting doesn't come with any notes and being a single parent is definitely tough. It is hard to manage all his needs by myself, especially whilst working and studying.

But it's worth all the difficult times when he laughs and smiles and says:

"Dad"

He has learnt how to blow kisses and melts my heart when he does.

Being a good dad is being there not only for the good moments but for the sleepless nights and the difficult times. It's also about being there emotionally whenever they need you.

After giving birth I decided to go ahead with my medical transition. Testosterone definitely changes you mentally and physically. It can be tough controlling all these hormones that are going on in your head, but I always find a way to manage.

I feel one step closer to the man I see myself as.

Being a trans and gay dad can be isolating as there aren't many people in the same position, and mostly they live in other cities, counties and countries. But I have made so many online friends.

Knowing that there are others going through the same thing all over the world, makes you feel like you're not alone. It helps to be able to talk to someone who knows exactly what it's like.

I wouldn't have been able to make this journey without the massive support behind me, especially at my lows in life. I am very thankful to you all.

Support wise, I have my family and friends, but mainly I am my own support. I am the one pushing myself for more and more. I have many goals for my future:

Surgery

Buying a home

Achieving my degree

I push myself because I want to make Gray's life the best it can be. I often get asked about if I want more children. Right now I want to focus on me and on my son.

I have Gray and he is amazing.

Alex Johnson

@daddy_to_gray

Chalk and Cheese

My twin girls are not the same,

The cliché is so very lame.

Evie's curls are oh so brown

And Amelie wears a golden crown.

Their differences don't stop there:

It is so much more than just their hair.

When Amelie smiles her eyes go thin,

And Evie has a great big grin.

What about the first words they said?

This will put the argument to bed:

Amelie shouted mama clearly,

Evie said dada, whom she loves so dearly.

What about the food they eat,

Surely they love the same old treats?

Alas no, even with the food they munch,

They differ with their favourite lunch.

Evie loves it served on bread,

Amelie is not so easily fed.

Evie loves her puddings sweet,

And Amelie is a fan of meat.

What about the games they play?

Twins girls play the same you say.

I have to say this isn't true,

There are loads of clashes with things girls do.

Evie quietly sits down to read,

Dancing is all our Amelie needs.

I have to say when all is done,

Both twin girls are rather fun.

And even though they're miles apart,

Raising twins is such an art.

I wouldn't change what has unfurled

Raising twins is my world.

Joe Elliott

Welcome to the World

I waited 9 months to see you without feeling you grow
But I already fell in love with you.

When you came to this new World
I held you in my arms, my miracle baby
At that precious moment you changed my life forever
I became a daddy of a wonderful little girl.

I held you in silence, skin to skin and heart to heart
In tears of my happiness and with the feeling of love.

Tamas Dominko

Nurture vs nature: no contest

I never knew the answer to nurture vs nature

I never knew my life was missing extra heartbeats

I never knew those heartbeats were the answer to my question

But then they arrived, one after the other.

My heart swelled and swelled again.

Extra heartbeats born to another but destined to be mine.

Surely this would answer that age-old question

Surely now I'd know what life was meant to be.

We weighed each other up.

Two personalities tiptoeing around each other.

Getting to know each other.

Learning to love each other.

But the extra heartbeat was overpowering.

It made the heart grow stronger and fuller.

And without even realising

Our two personalities merged.

Then along came number 2

A different beast altogether.

A new personality

The tip-toeing started again.

We fought, we struggled, we jostled for position.
But the extra heartbeat kicked in once more.
The heart swelled again, fuller and stronger
And the merging crept in quietly.

I see me in both of you
Every day, more and more.
It matters not who you were born to
You are mine.

The question is answered.
Completely and undoubtedly.
No contest.

Chris Gilbey-Smith

I heard the news of your graduation into parenthood and it stopped me with a deep glowing joy; my heart sang with reverent resonance.

For me, some of life's greatest learning has come from being truly intimate with a creature that perceives without category, has no capacity for dishonesty, and is unburdened by thought. A state of being as a mountain peak from which we have journeyed, and to which we can look back upon, with these new arrivals as our inspiration and our guides, reminding us of what it was to be there.

Cuddle them, kiss them, and hold them tight in the night. Love is a felt thing; touch and song; movement and light. Learning to be gentle and kind from us as their foundations; we are the giants on whose shoulders they will stand tall and mighty.

Rest when you can, body and mind, and spend time beginning to clear the weeds from the garden of your life, your child will need the space in greater and greater amounts as they grow.

Look into the blackness of their eyes as much as you possibly can, for as long as you possibly can, and you will know why once you do.

Bob Newton

Am I doing it right?

The lonely road of fatherhood seems just that at times. Lonely.

You're like a third wheel of a new relationship. An afterthought, trying to find your place.

Trying to do the same things, well ..., just as well.

The feeling of social inadequacy or parental incapacity.

The pressure to immediately feel connected to the baby, but you've not held that baby for nine months.

Sure, you might not feel like you have a role at all sometimes, but scratch beneath that just a little.

If you're not caring for your child directly, does that mean you don't care?

It turns out the road isn't actually that lonely at all.

Caring indirectly might be your job for a while and that is just as important.

It's the domestic version of "paying it forward" but you get something back everyday.

Ignore the noise for a moment, hold that child and feel everything else just drift away.

The noise disappears and you're in that moment.

You're everything that your child needs you to be.

They don't care if you're sweeping streets or raking in cash, drive an old banger or the latest release.

They care that you're there.

Arms open then closed around them. That you're patient, kind, loving.

Eight minutes or 18 years. Take a single moment. Shut out everything but that moment. Live in it. See how lonely it isn't.

If you still do that as they grow, and still live in that moment, then you've done something right.

Bradley Bruce

A Letter to the Future

Laying together skin on skin,

The humbling adventure of a lifetime begins,

A challenge, a quest, the most worthwhile test,

A blessed chance at fatherhood, I'll do my best,

To raise a daughter in this unpredictable world,

To teach her lessons to allow her wings to unfurl.

My oath to you, oh, beautiful Sienna:

To teach you Empathy so you connect emotionally with humankind,

To teach you Love so happiness and guidance is never hard to find,

To teach you Independence so there are no obstacles you cannot overcome,

To teach you Dedication so failure is never considered an option,

To teach you there are no glass ceilings, no boundaries, no limits on your potential,

Because a life filled with joy, happiness and self-worth is not just important, its essential.

Before the sun sets on this journey we call life,

I pray I can look back with nothing but pride,

To have raised a daughter with strength, knowledge and courage,

Whose imagination is limitless, passion unfiltered and dreams left to flourish,

As the world turns, I can get distracted so you may not always have my attention,

But my thoughts always circle back to you, my daughter, my heaven,

And while I may not be by your side forever,

Every moment spent with you I will treasure,

If you read this at some point in your life's adventure,

Know that being your father has been an honour that words cannot measure.

Vj Claire

All I Want

Draw Nanny Pat on the etch-a-sketch,

Throw my dolly and let's play fetch.

Pick the bogey off my finger,

Paint Mr Potato Head, make him ginger.

Look at my bottom; it smells yucky,

Buy the bread to throw at ducky.

Fix the toy leg so it stops whirring,

Smash the toy cat so it stops purring.

Pick me up but upside down,

Paint your face and be a clown.

Make this plate into a hat,

Draw Peppa Pig, no, not like that.

Wipe my bottom when I touch my toes,

Flick mummy's nose when she dares to doze.

Understand me when I start shouting,

Carry me about on every outing.

Let me comb your missing hair,

Pick my toy up way back there.

Wipe my nose when it starts dripping,

Patch me up when clothes start ripping.

Hold me tight to make me smile.

Always go that extra mile.

Most of the time just be there,

All I need is to show you care.

Give me kisses when I feel sad,

All these things make you my dad.

Joe Elliott

Adieu my son

He spoke to me in my sleep last night,
He said he had made a mistake.
It wasn't supposed to end like this
He just wanted to take a break.

He spoke again the other day,
He knew that all along
His life had crashed around him
And he wasn't worth a song.

How do we move on from this,
Will time just pass us by?
I think about him every day
I'm glad that I can cry.

I'll never see my son again
And that's the crying shame,
Each day I hurt with so much pain
I feel that I'm to blame.

Chris Jones

You never win

Dads,
When children bad
Dinnae be mad
And you'll be glad

You kept the heid
When indeed
Your nerves were shred
'Early bed'

You yell.
And, with look of hell
They troop
Without a look

Upstairs to rooms
Amongst the brooms
To bed
Unfed

But never fear
Your ones so dear
Place a bet
And conspire to get

Another chance

But not quite yet

While ire high

And sure enough

(It's master stuff)

With timing right

And eyes so bright

They tip toe down

To act the Clown

'Who me?'

Soon you'll see

It wisnae me

-Twas a flea

Oan ma nose

That made me rose

And shout

About

Naw, wisnae me

Anither chance

Jist wan mair chance

We'll be good

While guests scoff food

You'll never even

Ken we're here

As you sink

Yer beer

'Last chance then'

Dads cry oot

As weans' eyes blink

And toes they twink

Then slide down

Having won the crown

And nodding see

Each other's glee

Then cosy make

To dig and partake

Of the Show

No longer on

The floor below

John Doohan

Words On Fatherhood

I suffered my first ever panic attack at thirty years of age and I didn't have a clue what was happening to me. It was the day my son was born. I remember the whole room changing after 22 hours of labour and felt guilty that the attention was on me when it should have been on her as she was so tired at this point.

My wife Michelle was taken to theatre for an emergency C-section and I honestly thought she was going to die. I was terrified. I had experienced so many dark things in my life while working in secure units but nothing worse than thinking the people you care about so much could be gone.

Thankfully, both Michelle and my son survived but sometime later, we realised Michelle was suffering from anxiety and depression. During this period, I experienced nightmares about Michelle and Ethan dying in the theatre. I would wake up thinking it was real. Sadly, Michelle went on to develop severe post-natal depression and my world changed forever. I now know it could have been a mixture of things, including birth trauma for Michelle. I had never known anyone with the illness. I was so uneducated about mental health I used to wonder: 'how can people be depressed?' Within weeks of Michelle's diagnosis, I had to give up my job to care for Michelle and Ethan. I had loved the social side of my job and I was totally isolated.

Sometimes I would not get out the front door for days. Within months, my personality totally changed, and I was drinking in an attempt to cope with my racing mind which I could not stop, which impacted on my sleep even more during this stressful time.

I became angry. It got to the point where, if I did manage to get out with friends, I wanted to fight the doorman. I had this strange need to get hurt to try and stop what I was feeling and the thoughts that were going through my head.

I began to have uncontrollable suicidal thoughts, but never acted on them.

At the time, I felt like I couldn't talk to anyone. I was raised in a working-class community where my father and grandfather were coal miners. Growing up we looked up to 'hard men' who didn't show their emotions and now I was feeling emotional – and I was feeling weak. I kept telling myself I just had to 'man up' and everything would be okay.

It was difficult not knowing how long my wife would be unwell for. In the end, it took around eighteen months before she started to feel better, and of course, it affected our relationship. It so often causes the breakdown of families when there is no early intervention. I did not feel I could tell my wife how I was feeling, and I did not want to risk it impacting on her mental health.

I also did not want it on my medical records as I loved working and providing for my family. I suffered in silence for years. And then, my mother, who I loved so much was diagnosed with cancer.

My dark thoughts and nightmares worsened. For months, I had been lying to Michelle and telling her I was going to work but in fact I was isolating myself from people. I felt totally alone.

One day, whilst sitting in my car before walking into work, I had a complete breakdown. I literally just broke down and had no choice to get the help and now know that the quicker the help, the quicker the recovery.

Today from a bad experience I now used that experience in my life to help others while changing how we as organisations should be asking all parents regardless of gender as more support should be in place for same-gender parents, stay-at-home dads, single fathers, who as a result will have far better outcomes for themselves, family and the development of the child.

Mark Williams – Speaker, Author and Campaigner

Dads and partners

Becoming a Father is arguably the biggest transformation a man can ever experience in life and one that is little supported. Expectations are high (yours, your partners and your families, friends and work), and if those are not met (they rarely are), the reality can hit hard and bring up intense emotions. It is both exquisite and painful, and brings euphoric highs with depths a man has never experienced. A father is expected to feel like a father instantly, but he may not feel this for much longer, and that can be an uncomfortable place to be. He may feel anger and resentment, and yet be drawn to protect and provide. The ambivalence of still being required to fulfil the role of father, lover, businessman and friend is a tricky juggle and yet, there is often the idea that to talk about it being too much is a weakness, or worse.

What if we educated young boys at school how to be open about their feelings and sit with their emotions more than to man up and sweep those feelings away in shame?

What if we taught young men to understand that their intrusive thoughts can be normalised just by talking about them?

What if we showed men that it's okay to not be okay every day in every way and conditioned ways to find mental as well as physical resilience and strength to manage the challenges of becoming a parent?

Here are my top tips to dads to be and new dads:

If you can, maximise time off and try staggering your return to work if you can.

Life as a couple:

Most importantly, have an understanding that your relationship will change, possibly for the better, however, with tiredness, birth recovery and a baby (and all the gubbins) in between you, it will help to be more mindful of new ways to find intimacy and support.

Lowering expectations and being super sensitive are a bonus.

Talking: you may find it hard to talk much, but keep the communication going; keep it light if you can, and remember that laughter triggers an endorphin (your feel-good factor!) response.

Closeness: sometimes, words are not needed. A hug, a smile, eye contact and a hand-hold may be all that's needed.

Expect stress and tiredness levels to rise, and your normal ways of coping after a long day, changed. Try to counter-balance this by taking it back to the basic things you enjoy, talking to friends, gentle exercise or walking to clear your head.

Connect with your baby; now is a perfect time to have skin to skin with your baby, (partner and other kids too), carry them in a sling/baby carrier, massage or bathe them. Explore their little fingers and toes, the softness of their skin and make eye contact with them as you gently get to know them in your own time, your way. Communicate using soothing words or song. Find your tenderness.

Expect that you will have differences of opinion from your partner, but be prepared to listen to them too. They will be super exhausted and may not be making sense to you, but they will be instinctually navigating a new terrain and there's no manual. Respect that you may disagree over the best path to take at times.

Tiredness and vulnerability can be ugly at times. Expect the worst in this case and it may not be bad at all. With permission, hold the baby and encourage your partner to rest as often as you can. She may be trying to do it all herself to take the pressure off you, but will get exhausted quickly this way. Try and find a balance for you both. Nurture your relationship and think of novel ways to enjoy time together. Tip: it's the small gestures and the little things that matter. Document this time so you can look back a year down the line and beyond, and feel connected and nurtured again and again.

Eat well. Cook or order in nutritious meals and treat yourself and your partner. Now is an ideal time to drop standards slightly, get cosy and shut the world out for a while.

Don't be the hero: if you try to do it all and overload yourself, you will burnout. That's a fact. Also, do your best not to compete with your partner about sleep, or some me-time etc. Things can get toxic quickly if this happens. The huge "To Do" list for a perfect everything can wait.

You may need to drop some of the extra-curricular activities you've been doing to show solidarity/team-work. Same goes for booze and smoking. Cut back as much as you can. You will reap the rewards in the long run. This doesn't mean stop having fun and seeing friends, but accept the fact it can't be how it was. Your partner needs your support - even if it doesn't feel like it at times.

Connect with new parents that have everything in common with you at the moment: a baby!

Recognise your little achievements every day. Come from a place of gratitude and avoid wishing things were different somehow. This is it. How it is, right now. So instead of fighting it, comparing with others, or feeling disappointed in the things that haven't gone how you expected, do what you can to reframe those thoughts and feelings. Be present, aware and in each moment with a sense of gratitude and awe. It helps to write things down when the thoughts and feelings become overwhelming. Failing that, talk it out.

Sometimes it helps to talk to a pro: someone who can hold a non-judgmental space for you to be heard. You can feel emotionally held in those moments and let go of any pent up worries or fears you feel you can't discuss with your partner, family or friends. Getting support this way is not a weakness, it's a strength and a sensible, caring thing to do.

Sophie Burch – The Mamma Coach and founder of Beyond Birth

https://www.themammacoach.com

Hands On Dads — Deepening connection and increasing bonding for fathers

Touch is one of the most powerful ways to communicate love, deepen connection and promote relaxation for fathers and children. As humans, we are social creatures, hard wired to seek physical contact, acceptance in social groups and a sense of belonging to support our emotional, mental and physical health. We thrive on social connection; isolation and rejection can cause trauma, repressed feelings and emotional triggers that last a lifetime and influence how we form relationships and how we view ourselves. How we are loved and accepted influences how we love and accept ourselves and others.

Touch is our first method of communication. Babies and young children cultivate a sense of safety and security through being physically close to their parents. Secure attachment, which is the foundation of emotional and mental health, is encouraged and built through consistent acts of love which experientially teach children that they are loved, seen, heard and belong. It's the daily cuddle, bedtime story, nurturing massage, eye contact, being carried, hand-holding and head stroking that helps children feel part of a loving family where they are valued, respected and included. This builds trust and self-worth, which in turn encourages self-love and self-esteem. In the first few months of life, touch more than hearing, sight, or smell is how babies learn about the world and form meaningful relationships with those around them. Babies are able to sense how their parents feel about them by the manner in which they are touched (Field, 2001). Touch speaks the truth of love and emotion. It connects and anchors us in the moment to feel truly seen, supported and safe.

Fatherhood is an emotional transition for men, and yet it is not treated in this way. Feelings around fatherhood are not shared in the same way as feelings around motherhood. Many men enter into the unknown without a guide, feeling lost and alone. There is evidence that fathers may feel restricted in their opportunities to form a close attachment with their babies in the early days after birth, which can increase parent-related stress (Anderson, 1996b; Palkovitz & Palm, 2009; Pardew & Bunse, 2005) This lack of opportunity to "feel" into fatherhood can come from the ideas around traditional mother and father caring roles, choices around feeding, sleeping and general baby care plus the dynamic between the mother and father.

There is a lot to navigate in the early days of having a baby and as the post-natal period has been traditionally seen as female-led, fathers can feel left out, unsure where to find support and solace and often feel excluded. New fathers are bombarded with mixed expectations and cultural stereotypes around what it is to be a man and a father whilst adjusting emotionally and mentally to parenting and managing all the emotions that this unleashes. There is a lot to process and very little support, which can lead to stress, feelings of unworthiness and abandonment in their relationship with their partner. Add to this shaming around men expressing their emotions and being vulnerable, the experience can feel less than blissful, which in turn can induce feelings of guilt. A negative shame/judgement cycle can begin that can be destructive for everyone. The result of this is stress, which is harmful to father, baby and family.

It's time to make a change and create space for fathers to explore and express their feelings and emotions without shame and judgment in a safe place. Creating a daily connection ritual for fathers with their children can provide special bonding time and give support to a mother to allow her to practice self-care. Parenting shared is love shared.

A beautiful practice to encourage this is nurturing touch and baby massage, and studies have shown that its practice can be powerful in relieving paternal stress and increasing connection. Scholz and Samuels' (1992) study of fathers participating in baby massage showed that fathers appeared to thrive on the emotional and motivational benefits of the increased opportunity to touch their infants. Cullen, Field, Escalona, and Hartshorn (2000) found fathers who massaged their infants were more expressive, warm, and accepting in their interactions with their infants. A recent study undertaken by Darrell Cheng, Volk, Marini (2011) found that learning baby massage decreased paternal stress and that fathers may benefit from post-natal education.

Mothers and Fathers are of equal importance to their children. They both need emotional, mental and practical support. Their needs are not the same but are equivalent and vital for health and wellbeing. Happy connected relationships start with acceptance, trust, honesty and understanding. Touch connects us all and is the universal language of love.

Gayle Berry – Founder of Blossom & Berry and expert on parent and baby emotional and mental wellness.

Affirmations for love and nurture

"I am filled with profound love and gratitude for my partner. This baby is a beautiful love story between my partner, our baby and me."

"I set my own fears aside and focus on welcoming and nurturing a new life into our family."

"I intuitively know how to support my partner, in the way that she needs.

I take time to connect with my partner and my baby."

"I accept that this time is uncertain, but I choose to love and hold my partner and my baby, creating a safe space for us all."

"I lower my expectations and rise to the challenges of being the parent that I can be."

"I am all they need and I am good enough."

"Sometimes all I need to do is listen and see."

"I take time to tune into my needs and communicate them to my partner."

"I choose to slow down and observe my emotions as they arise."

"I am a capable, confident, compassionate parent."

"I know this will pass, so I take time to pause, notice and bank each moment I can."

"This time is about us and no-one else; I choose to trust in my inner wisdom."

Sophie Burch – The Mamma Coach and founder of Beyond Birth

https://www.themammacoach.com

Love and gratitude for this book

To all the fathers who contributed to this book, for sharing their vulnerability and their voices. I am honored to share your words and feelings.

To Mark Williams for his support and his words for this book, and Sophie Burch for contributing her wisdom on mental wellbeing for parents before and after birth.

Much gratitude to Peter Traynor for helping to bring this book to life by helping me with proofreading and organisational skills.

This book was written during COVID 19, which has been a challenging time for parents and for maintaining good mental health. Parenting presents limitless opportunities for joy and connection but also brings challenges and triggers. Children reflect the love in our hearts and also the fear that we hold about ourselves, our relationships and the world we live in.

Blossom & Berry believe that love creates love. Love always starts with you. As we love, care and nurture ourselves, we have a greater capacity to love others and to ultimately love the world forward. It's time to teach love and heal pain through creating connected loving relationships across the world.

With all my love as always,
Gayle
2020

Afterword on love....

What if?

What if it was actually easy?

What if we accepted we are loveable and loved?

Always held, guided and supported.

What if we recognised that our capacity to feel fear is also our capacity to feel love?

What if we realised we can't go wrong?

There is no right, should or perfect way only the way we choose and that opens up for us.

What if we just let go and saw ourselves reflected in everyone else?

If we saw the newborn baby inside us all born to love, open to explore, connect and grow.

That no one knows what they are doing and most of us aren't even being.

What if we realised that our challenges and mistakes are our greatest lessons?

That we are never alone as love is always there for us.

That suffering is all in our mind and that freedom lies in trust and surrender.

What if we realised that the story we play in our heads is just a story and we are the author and narrator?

That we can change the story, introduce new characters, change the plot and ending?

That pain is an illusion of the mind and love is the centre of peace.

That we can forgive others and still honour ourselves and be free of the need to cling to the familiarity of the pain of the past as comfortable and known.

What if we dropped all the resistance and just allowed ourselves to truly feel and be guided?

What if we stopped caring what others thought about us and we followed our feelings?

What if we fully expressed ourselves, honestly and authentically and fully in our truth?

What if we knew our learning would always be met with compassion, love and understanding?

What if it was easy?

What if we just love?

Giving Back

The profits of this book will be donated to the project Hub Of Hope as part of the charity Chasing The Stigma (Registered Charity No 1170757)

The Hub of Hope is the UK's go-to mental health support signposting tool, with more than 1,800 services listed. Since its launch it has directed more than 120,000 people to life-changing and life-saving help. It is free to download and use and free for organizations to register their details.

Available from the App Store, Play Store and via www.hubofhope.co.uk

Printed in Great Britain
by Amazon